Like Flamingos

(mostly) light-hearted poems (mostly) about life

Like Flamingos

Written & Illustrated by Corey Caskey

To the one I love, [identity withheld]

< Preface >

You, audience, please enjoy,
but a forewarning when reading this thing;
it has turbulent ups and downs,
like a teenager in a pubescent mood swing.

My first rhyme of many.

...[great] poems ahead.

Era

This is the era of...

...hold on, let me finish this text.

Colors

Jeffery has peculiar tastes.

His tongue constantly craves crayons.

But Jeffery is 54 and not a kid.

Seriously, what's wrong with this man?

Vasectomy

Snip snip, goes the doctor.
Be mature, dude, I say back.
You're slicing open my balls here.
Don't commentate, okay?

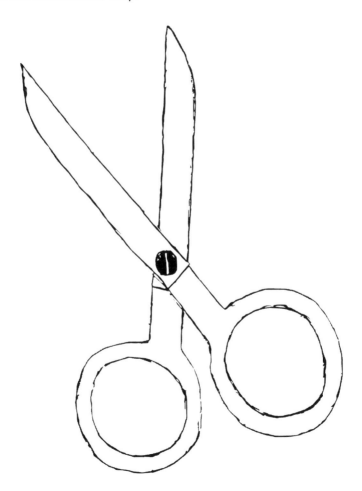

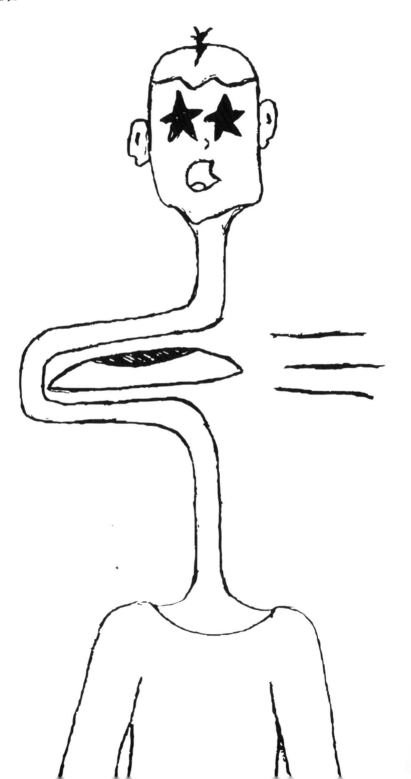

YouTube Star

I once dabbled at being a YouTube sensation,
engaging in elaborate and scripted narration.

Pretending to be a British survivor dude.
A kid buzzed on Red Bull with a new pair of shoes.
An injury-prone, nerdy gangster.
A gangly ping-pong player.
What a lame and turdy twerp I was.

I surely regret these decisions of mine –
ideas flowing from my childish mind.

I failed at denting this Great Wall of Vlogs.
And thanks to you, the kind, fairy-comment moths.
You loved suggesting that I was so fucking stupid.
I wish you the worst. Go. Please contract lupus.

My videos were terrible and completely unbearable.
A removal of eight years has provided some clarity
and allowed me to say with obvious sincerity
that I was never destined for camera stardom.
Maybe behind the safety of a Word document.

Rain

Mother Nature is promiscuous.
Thunder are her rumbling moans.
Lightning are her orgasmic bursts.
Rain are her reflexive surges.
And we dance in her puddles.

Three Wishes

If I had access to three free wishes,
then I could wish for something vicious.
I would ask for a magical pair of scissors
to cut off the man-buns of asinine hipsters.

Fuck, those things are really ugly.
Keep your other two wishes, I say smugly.

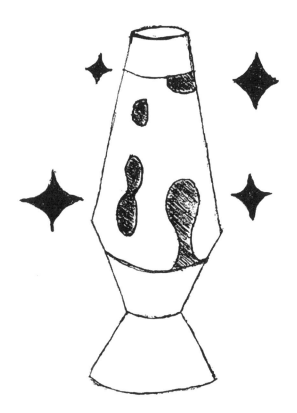

Band

For those who play music because they truly love it,
I applaud you.
You are an inspiration to me.
For those who do it for a shallower reason,
like a crush,
I don't applaud you,
but I understand your motives.
I was you.

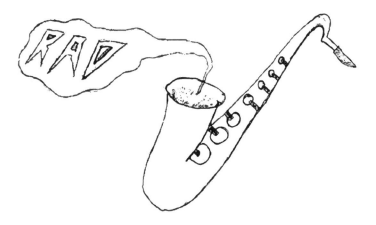

Of course, my crush ultimately decided not to join the band. But, because my parents had already shelled out hundreds of dollars for a saxophone, I was stuck playing it for the next three years. A simple reminder to all of you next time you want to do something out of lust.

Peaches & Eggplants

Peaches are round and savory and plump –
perfect to describe your girl's rump and dump pump.
Eggplants are weird, purple, dong-shaped objects.
But I liken my wiener to corn.
Then she can slob on my cob yet.

Father

I have a father who owns a legendary moustache,
while his son possesses only a penciled crustache.
From school, he's grown his for twenty-five years.
Flecked with gray, it's nestled between his two ears.

Mine has been thriving for nigh on two weeks,
sprouting lamely like dead grass from my cheeks.
While he slept, I shaved my father's hairy upper lip,
stealing his hard-earned label of proprietorship.

It wasn't out of jealousy or envy or greed.
I was just curious to see him without that brown weed.
But after seeing what he looked like with it gone,
I desperately glued those individual hairs back on.

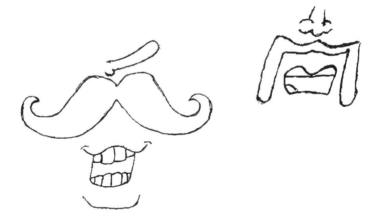

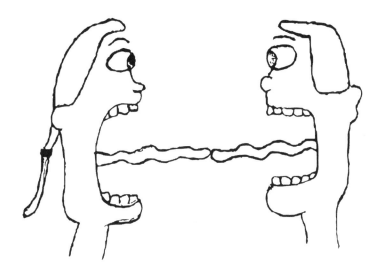

The Art of Kissing

Kiss me. Tease. Kiss me. Please.
I know your lips. I want a sip.
I pucker them shut and bring them near,
drawing them close against your ear.
Whisper something sweet –
something soulfully complete.
They trace your cheeks and down your neck,
dotting your skin with subtle bird pecks.
I touch your chin and pull you in,
closing the distance till we're breaths away.
Don't worry my love, I'm here to stay.
Kiss me. Long. Kiss me. Slow.

Cats

Cats are the assholes of the animal kingdom.

"Pussies" was too obvious.

Dogs

Dogs are bitches,
because some things are aptly named.

(I'm lying. All animals are gifts to humanity.)

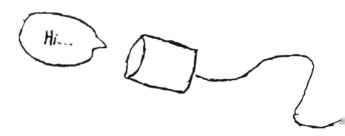

Long Distance

Long distance is the worst thing for a relationship,
especially one in its adolescent stages.
But, maybe, if you're strong enough
and committed enough, it works.

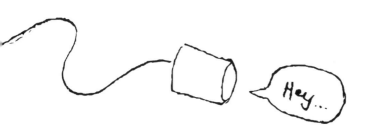

Trading

Give me twenty-five pennies. You'll get a quarter.

Give me a missile. You'll get a mortar.

Give me a news anchor. You'll get a reporter.

Bartering is stupid.

Thankfully we have money.

Intruder

An audacious squirrel entered my house –
more like trespassed on the premises –
presenting his middle claw in derogatory fashion
and sprinting beneath my legs.

What a mooch, exchanging the outdoor cold
for my free heating and decadent carpet.
Yes, please shit everywhere you
little, disease-infested rodent.
Prance around with my overweight cat if you want.
He'd crush your puny body if he sat on you.

I caught that twitchy bastard in a bed sheet
and wrestled him down.
Or, perhaps, he is a her.
I don't aspire to look for squirrel genitalia.
Its bulbous eye probed my soul and
told me it was about to fuck me up.

Clawing me, it ran out the door.
What an ass. I was just trying to help.
I named it *Scott.*

Beauty

You are far too beautiful to love, my mature, ruby rose.
I need to be the attractive one in this relationship.

Insecure

I'm insecure.

I need a blanket of compliments.

Tell me I'm good enough.

Tell me I'm worth it.

Tell me you love me.

And hope I believe it.

Life Lessons

Learn to love. Learn to live.

Learn to hope. Learn to give.

Learn to be human.

Learn to be true, man.

Learn to be you, man.

And when you've learned all you can,

teach.

King Crab

A group of rusty crustaceans
eat soup in a crusty bus station,
beside droopy and musty carnations,
trooping for the must-see coronation.

I Don't Know Loss

I don't know loss like that of some others.
I haven't lost a father, mother, sister, or brother.
My only loss is that of my caring grandmother.

Yet I have known loss like others know it.
It was unexpected, and it happened in an instant.
A week prior, I had been celebrating her birthday,
too engaged in my own endeavors to break away
and be present in our last moments together.

Then, just like that, she was gone,
while I'm left struggling to live on.
It's something I'll never forgive myself for.
I know loss forever more.

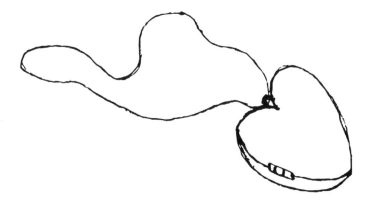

Whisper

I pray to die quickly and painlessly,
in a split second without thrashing or
choked out breaths or
witnessing things go dark.

I'd prefer to exit in the same way I arrived –
entirely anticlimactically,
not knowing it even transpired.

Disappearing like a whisper
or a soundless, scentless fart.

Afterlife

The afterlife is an imagined notion.
Not imagined as in fake.
Well, we don't really know until we get there.
It's shrouded in hypotheticals and belief.
We could be wrong. We could be right.

Or, hell, it might be nothing more than a queuing station,
manned by some old-lady, DMV-type clerk who
hands us index cards with red-inked chicken-scratch
telling us how we died.

We'd take a number from a grocery store dispenser.
Wait in line. Punch our card. Stamp our hand.
And be divvied up based on our type of death.

Some of you are car accidents.
Some of you are overdoses.
Some of you are...*autoerotic asphyxiations.*
Get used to that label. We'll be here for a while.

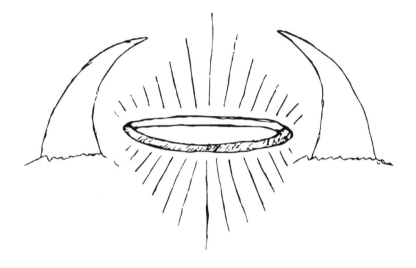

She

She is an unhinged feline defecating on my carpet.
She is a horned devil who draws my blood scarlet.
She seduces with her loose tongue like a harlot.
But I only see her as perfect and far from that.

Impressed Yet?

Girls aren't hard to decipher.

They all like buff guys.

Tough guys.

Trouser-cuff and chin-scruff guys.

Not us cream-puff guys with not enough thighs.

Gangly arms and bread-stale charm

can't compete with swagger smiles and styles.

I'm everything that's undesired, but I have money,

so, ladies, line up single file.

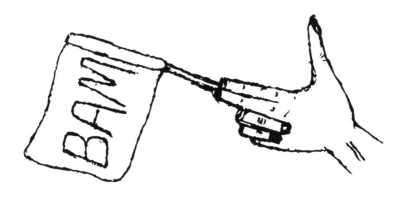

Finger Guns

Pew. Pew.

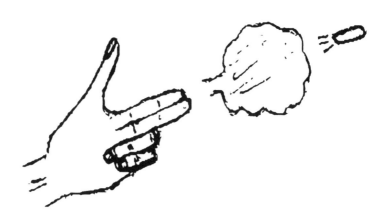

Genesis

You are the beginning of something marvelous.

Something inexplicably extravagant.

You are ceremonious like a chorus of trumpets.

Three Little Words

Everyone loves hearing those three little words.

They're on the tip of my tongue.

Come closer so I can whisper them to you.

Inhale my farts.

Genes

People ponder incredible things.
Galileo pondered the universe.
Newton – math and some other shit.
I ponder my personal qualities,
wondering where I got them.
I differ so greatly from my parents
that it mustn't be genetics.
Osmosis seems like a better explanation.

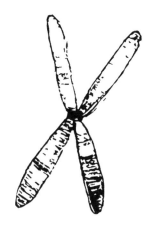

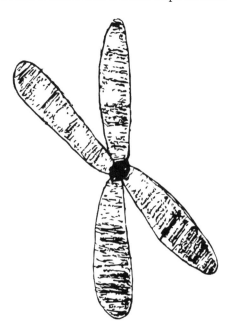

Jeans

Loose, boot-cut pants.
Tight, denim jeans.
You give me a quick glance
and tell me to try the tweed.
Yeah, they don't have my size.

Astrophysics

Star science.

Cool.

Let's try star biology

to figure out what's inside those fuckers.

Mitochondria, I hope.

That shit is bitchin'.

Body Shots

Everyone is given a purpose in life.
Mine is having a depression in my chest.
A concave to hold liquid, if necessary.
I could lie horizontal and use it as a cereal bowl.
Instead, I went to Red Robin
and let old women do body shots out of it.

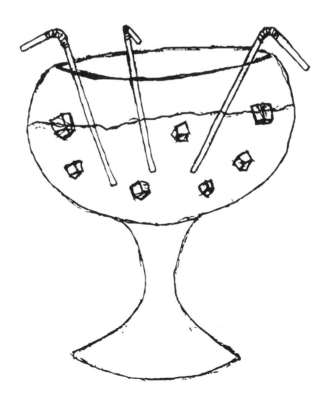

Stop Sign

A chicken crossed the road.

This is not the beginning of a joke.

Without stopping, it sauntered to the middle.

It squatted on the double yellow lines, taunting traffic

and disregarding – no, disrespecting – that stop sign.

Damn, did I think that chicken was badass.

I wanted to be like it.

I grabbed the PRNDL stick like I was…

…ah, this is no time for similes.

With my foot against the gas pedal, I floored it in reverse

because, if anything, I was too far over the white line

and didn't want to get in trouble.

I felt badass for doing the law-abiding thing.

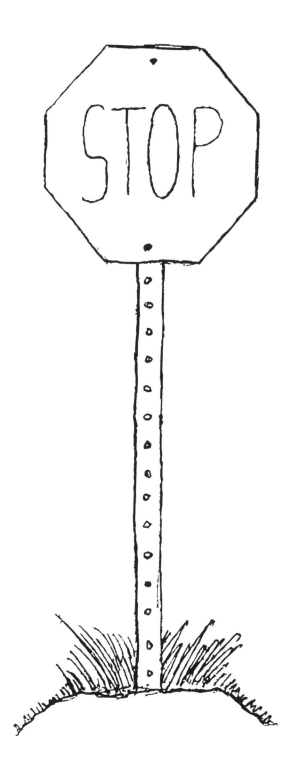

Passions

I was "the man" in fourth grade,
turnstiling my way through women.
Each week, I struck up a new courtship.
Nothing ever happened, though.
I was merely a child, you pervs.
But, thankfully, that pattern didn't carry
over to my teenager years.

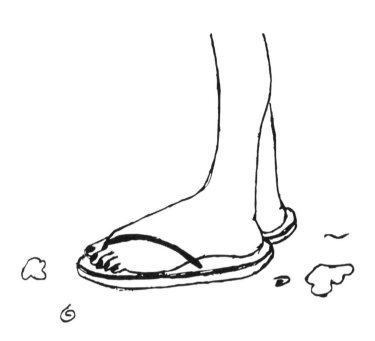

College Dorm Showers

Need I say more?

Yes?

...okay.

Pube-littered, skeet-covered, piss-coated coffins of disease.

Bring your shower flip-flops.

Throckmorton

I once created an imaginary animal for class.
A dragon-tentacled creature: indescribably badass.
It lacked a label but demanded a legendary name.
Nothing that sounded silly or ordinary or lame.

The internet helped me solve this pesky problem.
I unearthed *Throckmorton* – an unexpected gem.
I chose it because it flowed with a potent amount
of a daunting and beautifully haunting sound.

You're jealous, till we both find out what it means.
It's the curvature of one's thing tucked in his jeans.
So that's that.

Caught (Part I)

Arnold enjoyed slutty chicks and busty boobs,
with his computer storing all those lewd nudes.

His laptop sat open in the living room,
and what happened next made Arnold cower.
It came alive with dirty videos of cartoons
when his mom typed in his internet browser.

The entire situation was utterly embarrassing,
mostly because it was titled *Gentle Ass Kissing*.

Caught (Part II)

Arnold had grown up to be a normal teenager,
still maintaining his role as a dirty screen-player.
Hand in pants, he tugged hard on his ding-dong,
until, suddenly, his freshmen roommate came along.
His heart beat fast as he had almost been seen.
Jumping in bed, he stopped his depleted milking machine.

Caught (Part III)

Sex is super cool. Arnold is no fool.
He's finally found someone to love and to hump,
with a bosom sweet and booty ever so plump.
She and he are interlocked in a sweaty embrace,
fully engaged in the most innate bodily race.

They're so focused on staying quiet to avoid being caught
that anyone barging in was a forgotten afterthought.

His bedroom door swung open quite rapidly,
causing him and the girl to yell out frantically.
Holy balls, it was just the dog!
Phew.

When Nature Calls

Buttholes splurge our digested contents.
Toilets catch those discarded brown bananas.
I prefer the sanctity of my bathroom at home,
but, *twice*, things went south while driving
that I was forced to destroy some CVS stalls.
They lacked air freshener to cover the stench.
Enter at your own risk, you wandering customers
and other victims of diarrhea.

Pills

I lay out a bunch of pills every morning,
close my eyes, take one,
and wait to see what happens.

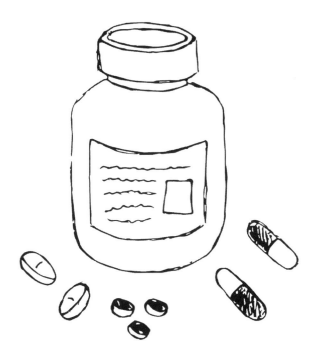

Today, I got an erection.
It was uncomfortable at my uncle's funeral.

Seven Months

Edward bet himself how long he'd not pet himself.
It was a stupid thought, but he totally sought to reset himself.
Some unworldly strength allowed him to last
for the eternity-perceived time of seven months pass.

He lost forearm strength with his junk at arm's length.
Without genitals being tickled by his tiny, thin fingers,
Edward would stare at girls and awkwardly linger.
The walls would ooze drooled seductiveness,
interfering with his mental productiveness.
Pillows moaned for his fleshed presence,
begging him to succumb to his hormonal adolescence.

As the seventh month closed, Edward had concluded
that he had been idiotic and painfully deluded.
It had been soooooo long and things had become numb.
He exploded one day after beating it like a drum.
Never again did Edward painfully refrain
from readily playing with his well-lubricated crane.

Cuffing Season

Winter is what lonely people call cuffing season.
When girls ask for dates, I make bluffing reasons.
No, that's a muffin-topped guy huffing n' sneezing.
I think I feel something: y'know, muffin queezing.
This poem was stupid. Toe hair toughing tweezing.

Sea Life

I had an idea. A simple idea.
It lacked the illuminated lightbulb and
the certain euphoria of eureka.
It seemed as ordinary a thought as any,
like it had been dormant in the back of my head
and finally swam upriver.
In a world where evolutionary tendencies
lead us to wanting multiple people,
I craved only one.
I tested the waters and met a few fish.
It didn't work out. Elusive creatures, they were.
Eventually, I landed on an exotic porpoise.
Why had I not thought about this earlier?
She'd stay with me for life.
She was the one.

Love metaphors. Wow.

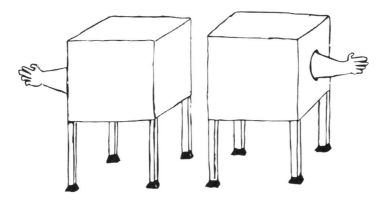

Magic

You must be made of magic or something,
she says.
No, just normal people parts,
I respond.

Depressed

Dark days are dark.
Bright days feel dull.
Smiles are deceptive.
Sunglasses mask my soul.

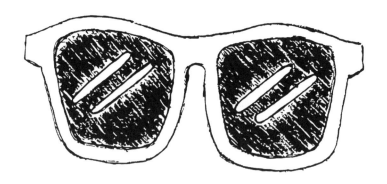

Text

I was left on read by a girl once.
I was upset, but, little did I know,
she had died later that day.
My luck.

Let Me Be Me

Don't tell me to be extroverted or different
when, inside, I don't want to be.
Don't throw your personality onto me and
think that I can be like you.

Sometimes I just want to give up on people and
seclude myself because that's natural for me.
I think I was made this way for a reason.
Though, I'm not really sure why.

I might feel differently had
I been given these social skills at birth.
But that thought passes.
I'd rather be like this,
and I won't change myself to please you.
I like the silence. I prefer my thoughts.
Your opinion doesn't interest me.
Sorry to be rude, but it doesn't.
Especially when it's about how I live.

Skype Date

Booty,

patooty,

gluties,

footies,

doodies,

the jamjams,

the gramgrams,

the wambams,

jammies,

those are jamjams,

din din,

delish,

poooooooooop,

International Women's Day...

...typing random things can take you anywhere.

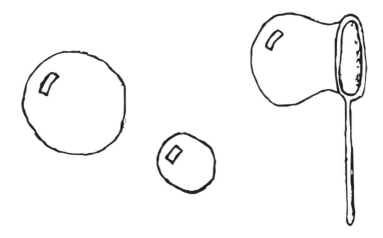

Perfect Poem

Perfect poems don't exist,
except in this book.
Blessed are those who are humble.

Just

She is his friend.
He is hers.
She sees his soft eyes.
He sees her sweet, shy smile.
She gives a lingering gaze.
He lingers back.
They like each other, but platonic rules
blanket their underlying feelings.
Just friends.

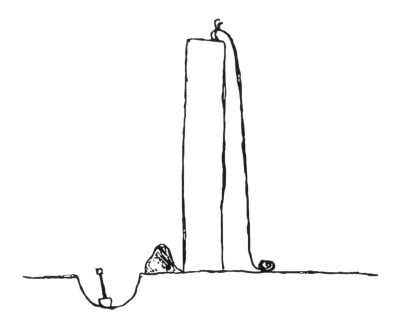

Life is a Fucked-Up Journey...lol

sup dude, what's happening?

nothing u?

just thinkin

wow u must rly be bored
what r u thinking bout?

life

oh shit. like what?

how life is a fucked-up journey

what does that mean?

y'know, it's rly a kick in the crotch
and sometimes a pat on the back

that makes sense

you never know what you'll get
out of a day or week or month

that sounds like forrest gump

dude focus
good things happen to bad people
bad shit to good people
loved ones die

srsly bro r u high?
where is this coming from?

...

what?

i stepped in gum
in my favorite shoes

haha
ur right life is a fucked-up journey

Names

Randall is a Randall.
Caroline is a Caroline.
Dominic is creepy but, nonetheless, a Dominic.

People always say you look like a Randall –
like a Caroline –
like you're constipated but, yes, like a Dominic.

And Randall and Caroline always respond,
"No shit, that's because it's my name."
Dominic, with his thick unibrow, says nothing.

You think, "Yeah, that's their name and their face.
They belong together."
You could see seventy Randalls or Carolines or Dominics
and come to the same conclusion.

But what if it were something different?
What if Randall changed his name to Phil?
Caroline to Beatrice?
Dominic to Dominic?
Because, apparently, he likes his name.

Would your brain still make the same association?
Or would names just become a meaningless label?

You're Not Unique

You think you're special or unique or any other
synonym meaning you're different in a good way.
Stop telling yourself that because you're not.

Anything you've done, somebody else already has.
And probably better, too.
Anything you've seen has been seen.
Anything you've thought has been thought.
You're not unique.

You're built on other people's accomplishments.
You just don't know it yet, but you will soon.
The odds are minimal that you're unique at all.
I could find your doppelganger and easily replace you.
You're not unique.

The mouth of my reflection mimics these words.

Jealous

My girlfriend – bless her heart – noted the cuteness
of a group of little boys at the bowling alley.
My ego wouldn't allow an outward concurrence.
Instead, I expressed my envy by punching
them all in their stupid, pudgy faces.
She was both thoroughly impressed and appalled.

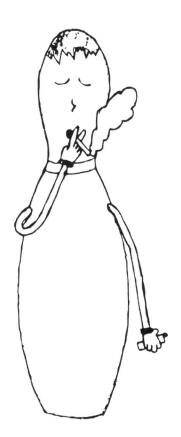

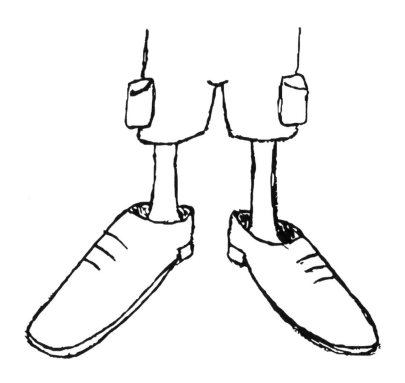

Life Only Gets Worse

Children don't understand the complexity of this world.

They see one foot in front of them, and that's it.

I want to yell at them to see more and understand more.

Know what I know! Grow up!

But I also don't want them to because life only gets worse.

Trust me, I would know.

I've seen it.

Golden Shower

There is no greater convenience
than peeing in the shower.
No greater freedom.
And it saves water, too.
Anyone who says they don't do this
is lying to your face.

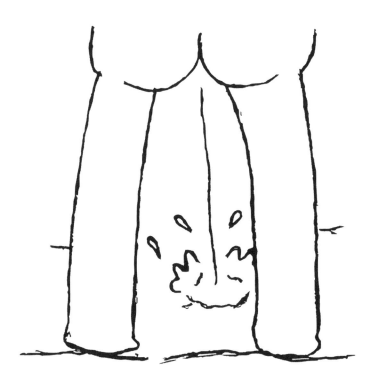

A Poem About Nothing

Far too often, poems are about nothing.
This one's no different. How dreadfully touching.

Tiny, magical fairies sprinkle us with moldy dairy.
They ran out of pixie dust and crumbled pizza crust.

The sky is a porous ceiling without any feeling.
Airplanes will crowd around its white fart clouds.

A perfect Christmas tree is a thing we run to see.
A giant, leafy root ultimately burned to black soot.

It's been a short journey, but we've learned a bunch.
Just kidding; we haven't. Now let's go get some lunch.

Simple Quiz

Let me ask you a few questions, if you please.

How do basketball players like their coffee?

Without a doubt, with some Kareem!

Correct! How do paper sales people make shirt sleeves?

With extra-durable, white paper reams.

You are quick-witted. When don't we love drugs the least?

When they finally hit our desperate bloodstream!

Three for three! When's a red-head at his brightest sheen?

While wearing extra-strength sunscreen.

You're doing absolutely splendidly!

Why do people like sleeping in the land of the free?

Of course, to have the American Dream.

And that's a wrap on this quiz to you from me.

Circus

Unfurl your luscious curls just like those other girls.
Let them fall down your supple cheeks and chin.
Pull me close to your shapely body so I can sink in.
You are my bearded woman.

Put on your plastic nose. It's red like a rose.
You look worse without your white makeup.
Your face will haunt my dreams if we ever break up.
Play with your fifty other clown car friends.

Swallow your pointy swords. They muffle your words.
They are elongated shafts, a pun I didn't mean.
Yet you choke on my small spacecraft,
something I can't quite glean.
Do you prefer metal to flesh?

You are my strong man. Don't get me wrong, man.

Hold me like a child and sing me a song, man.

Your arms are my warmth. Your legs are my support.

Take me places and be my escort.

Everyone loves a striped singlet.

I am your ringmaster,

with moustache twirled and greasy slick.

Enter our tent and watch our weird tricks.

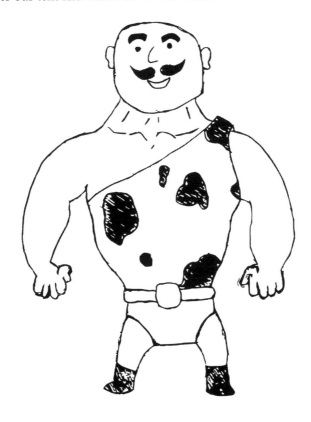

Pimples

I call pimples pimps,
and I have so many pimps
that I'm basically a hooker.

Let Me Serenade You

Whip it out and play that sexy saxophone.
Hearing those baritone notes, she blasts a moan.
That golden horn reaches maximum tones
of blissful silence
because I don't really know how to play.
It's like an impossible-to-understand science.
I don't know what else to say.

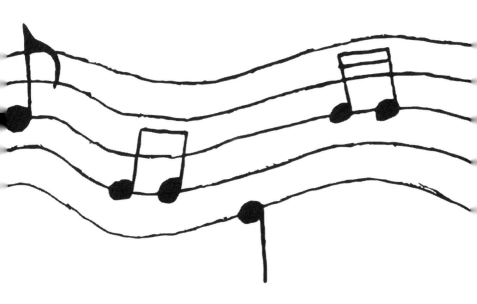

Euthanize

Clarice invited her friends over one evening for a typical gabby gal sleepover. Makeup. Gossip about boys. Other bullshit I don't know about because I, as the narrator, am a guy. Clarice's dad wanted to fit in – youthanize himself, per se. He stumbled into the living room shouting, "I'm a winner," for whatever reason. Being the uninformed person he was, instead of throwing up a W with his hands, he used the Shocker to represent his verbal proclamation. Snickers from her friends made Clarice cover her eyes. Poor Clarice.

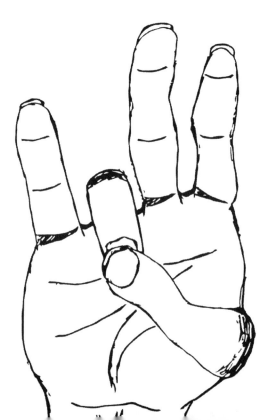

Confidence

Some guys pluck all the luck in the world,
those gucky, schmucky fucks.
Their creepy stares and greasy hair get them every girl.
They flaunt them and engage in nonchalant jaunts.

Their view is to woo and screw women
and accrue them in their queue as they please.
They have a capacity for tenacity
and audacity to steal kisses from them.
They tickle skin with their pickle thin
like some degenerative sleaze.

Unlike these cock-blocking, schlock-stocking jocks,
I'm a locked beanstalk with no four-leaf shamrocks.

A little lip kiss of brittle lip bliss with spittle and
a taste of Skittle in the middle are hard to come by.
I dream crazy schemes in teeming, steamy dreams
of how I can wow and plow her so now I vow to try.

The One-Legged Man

There once was a man who was one-legged,
perceived by everyone he met as such.
They would stare and point in fright,
and it was all because of his camo leg cast
and camo-print crutch.

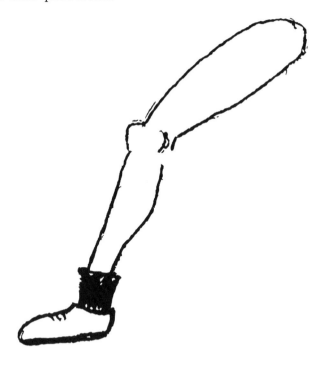

Smelling Bee

Marvin has an unfortunate diffusing problem.
When he's nervous, he farts the scent *Death of Autumn*.
A posterior stank. A methane drank.
Like he ran over a skunk (couldn't say skank).
He sat on stage amidst a murmuring crowd,
another fart rippling off his chair quite loud.
And that's how Marvin turned the spelling bee
into the first annual smelling spree.

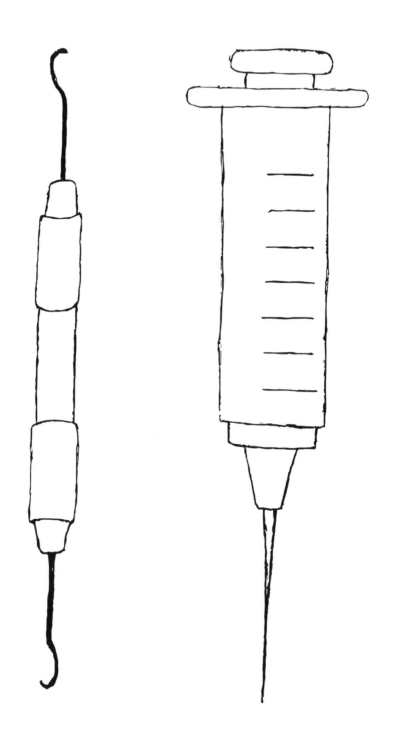

Probed & Prodded

I beg of you, stick your fingers in my mouth,
far in the recesses of it.
Talk to me and ask me questions like I don't have
a mouthful of your colorful, latex gloves.
Hear my gurgled responses.
Stare at me like I'm under a microscope.
Stretch my gums like some lump of playdoh.
Compensate me with a toothbrush?
What the shit.

Guide me and bend me over your sterile bench
covered by that thin paper shit.
Slide your lubed index finger into a place
meant only for exit. Not at all for entry.
Do it again because you didn't get a good feel the first time.
Jesus, doc, a third time?!
Are you really even a doctor?
No? Just some dude who bought a white lab coat?
Well, this was a waste.

Pixelated Love

I'm fairly certain that she loves me.

I surely hope that she thinks of me.

I discuss with her all the things that must be.

The way her eyes look, I believe she trusts me.

Though, I can't tell for sure 'cause she's stuck in my TV.

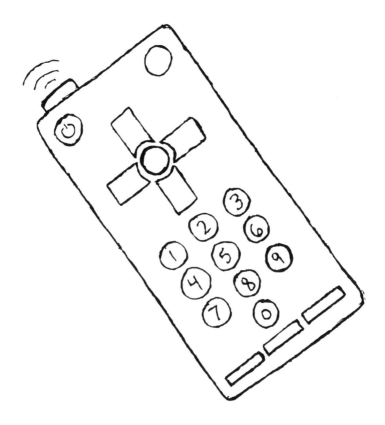

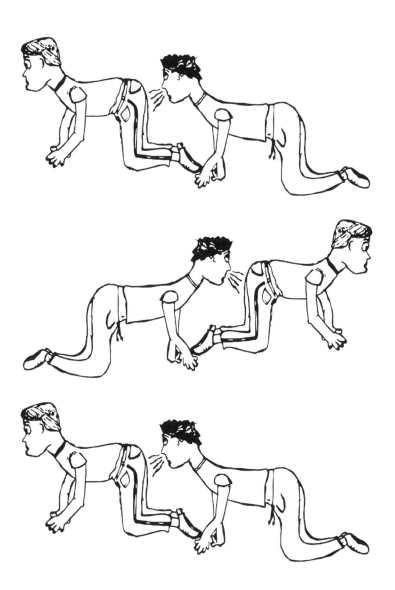

Brown

Brown seems to be the color of death and decay.

Bananas turn brown.

Apples and plants do as well.

I'm not sure what happens to corpses, though,

but I'd rather not see. I assume they're brown, too.

Who decided this anyway?

Why couldn't a cheerier color be associated with death?

Something to lighten the mood a little.

Tangelo, perhaps.

Commitment

Poems involve very little commitment.
Just as soon as they start, they end.
I like that.
No need for long, drawn-out writing.
That's why I don't write novels.
Just kidding, I do write those.
This is a plug for my upcoming book,
arriving sometime eventually.

Placemats

How desperate are you to put an ad on a placemat?
No one looks at those things.

Single Life

Carpeted walkways are worn from constant foot traffic.
Thick Plexiglas lines both sides of the hallway.
Blatant camera flashes scare away darkness.
Observations are scribbled on notepads.

Blockaded behind these windowed walls are "the singles."
The people untethered by anyone and anything,
milling about and living their lives.
Us "attached people" look on in confusion,
desperate to understand their erratic patterns.

Hidden Motives

I don't go to parties to drink.
I woohoo a little.
I crank out some classic dad moves.
I pass off shots to get other people wasted.
Then I stand alone by the free food and eat.
No shame.

Personification

Succulent succulents
suck on subsequent supplements
from truculent covenants
of plucky, crewmen gents.

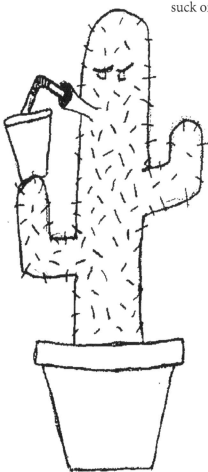

Off Day

Put shaving cream on those eyeballs.

Put toothpaste on those armpits.

Put nasal spray on those toes.

Put fungal cream on that tongue.

Do These Things

Cry to me, and I'll build you a pool to catch your tears.
Share your thoughts, and I'll write you a poem.
Relinquish your love, and I'll treasure you till death.
Tell me a secret, and I'll carry it with me forever.
Wish to a star for anything, and I'll make it come true.
Do these things, and I'll do them all for you.

Rumors

Immature people love to spread rumors.
They're insecure about themselves and desperate
to put others down to make themselves feel better.
I would never do that.
By the way, did you hear that Martha's a big 'ol slut?

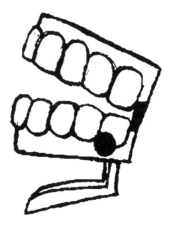

Shame

Next time you masturbate,
think about all the dead people who are
probably watching you.
That'll kill the mood.

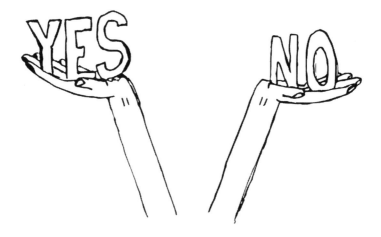

Love Thy Parents

Yeah, I suppose you could call them cool.

On one hand, they have super strict rules.

They have dreary life lessons and curfews and chores.

On the other hand, they pay for most the stuff I ask for.

So, eh, maybe.

I'm still on the fence.

Behind The Curtain

Some theories suggest our lives are simply a video game,
which makes me think how stupid that sounds.
What all-powerful being or extraterrestrial thing
would want to play my life? Or your life?
Or most people's lives?
They're all so ordinary.
But when I remember we have the Sims,
it no longer seems so farfetched.

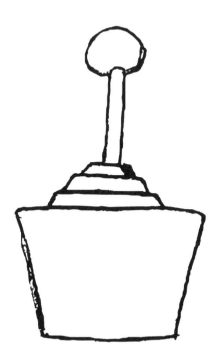

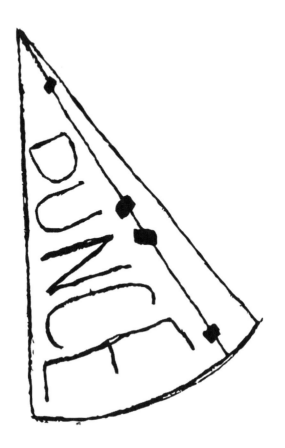

I Double Dog Dare You

Call me an idiot.

Say it to my face and see what happens.

Okay, you're an idiot.

...

Ah fuck, you called my bluff.

Irony

There was a random drug search at my high school.
Being "funny" and a little uppity, I joked,
"What if I got caught?"
knowing damn well that I've never done drugs.

Five minutes later, my teacher received a call
requesting my presence in the front office.
Some dog smelled drugs in my car.
Well, fuck me in the ass,
which is not where I store my imaginary drugs.
Ironic isn't it.

Snow Days

Snow days are magical.

Frozen, white crystals falling softly,

kissing the ground, each other, and our faces with cold lips.

We disrupt the beauty of this perfect dandruff coating.

We take pictures of us throwing it

or dancing around in it

or looking up with our tongues out to catch a few.

I don't participate, so I can distance myself and say this.

That look-up-and-stick-out-your-tongue thing, yeah,

it looks like you're preparing for a wiener in your mouth.

Just letting you know.

PENIS

SNOWMAN

Indescribable Pain

Come talk to me about pain when you've tasted
shoe leather or tennis ball felt or knuckled bone
against your balls at a high velocity.
You will be stuck in a limbo of numbing pain
and nausea and tears in what can only be
summed up as HOLY FUCKIN' MOTHER OF GOD!

Or if you've pushed a person out of your body,
we can talk, too.

Shower Thoughts

The best thoughts are shower thoughts.

What some might call power thoughts.

Always avoid those sour thoughts.

Have those sexy, every-hour thoughts.

Empty Thoughts

Troubling are those empty thoughts,

buzzing around my smarts like pesky moths.

Their mouths are full of my ideas like heavy froth.

Now my brain moves as slowly as a steady sloth.

My empty thoughts mined me down to an empty mind.

Misunderstanding

Misunderstandings are tight-roped situations –
inevitable implosions if not handled properly.
Say the wrong thing and suffer the consequences.
Say the right thing and don't suffer them.
It's a pretty dichotomic, black-and-white notion.

Except for those exceptions that pop up randomly.
Like mine. Let us begin.

A single Lego rested in its soon-to-be-perceived
precarious, "rightful" position centered between me
and another kid.
I picked it up, as it had no label, physical or otherwise.
At least, not the one this other kid apparently saw,
claiming it as his possession.

Delicious, metallicy blood drained down my throat
and stained my teeth after I received a mouthful of fist.
Really? You punched me over a fucking Lego?

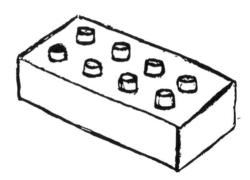

Hey, You

Oh, I know you! You're that guy from that thing.
Your name hides somewhere, but it just won't ring.
We both know it'll be awkward if I say I forgot,
so I use ambiguous words like *man* or *sport* or *hot shot.*
I try to avoid guessing your painfully elusive name,
until you leave me alone with my armpits of sweat shame.
Oh wait, I think I got it! It has to be Don or John or Ron?
Forget it, you turned around, and you're now too far gone.

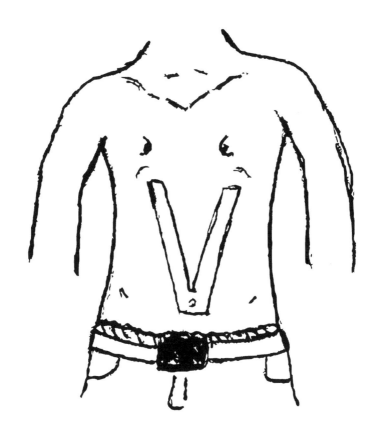

The Virgin

Being a virgin is underrated
because sex is overrated,
says the guy who has never had sex and
clearly doesn't know that it feels mind-blowing.

The World I Live In

I live in an entangled world,
noosed by its cat's cradle of flawed logic.
I live in a world of "we're all winners."
Where first and last are both synonyms for best,
and best has purged itself hollow.

Dedication, my dad told me, is essential.
Achievement isn't some handout or free sample.
Yet my generation disagrees.
No wonder we're considered soft and lazy.

I live in a world of free and impassioned speech.
It's beautiful and elegant, in theory.
We can express ourselves and say what we please
and inspire others.
But, somehow, things became broken and askew.

We've become so offended easily,
and it's become so easy for us to enjoy offending.
I want free-thinkers who topple ignorance
and fight those who wait to reattach the ropes
no longer tethering us to stupidity.

These people love nothing more than chaos.
But they should really be helping save us. Now.

I live in a world where left and right aren't directions.
They are sides of a war amongst ourselves.
Taking a stance results in missed connections.
I live in a world where the middle is a "backseat."
Where considering everyone's thoughts is ignorant.
Blind, undying loyalty is expected.

We need objective, intelligent people.
They will restore this world.

I don't know how things ever got so fucked up.
The answer eludes me, but I cling to hope that it exists.
Until I find it, though, I am left in the world I live in.

Interlude

Phalluses falling, frantically frolicking.
A cascade of cocks cautiously coddling.
Wieners winding 'round her windpipe.
Dicks dropping down the dirty drainpipe.

Circle

Life quite literally comes full circle.
You start in diapers, and you end in them, too.
You struggle to move in both stages of existence.
You rely on other people to feed and bathe you.
You're forced to mash food with very few teeth.
And you're the treasures of this Earth.

The only differences between you two
are supreme, smooth skin
to the wrinkled dust constantly flaking off;
and the hopefulness of life ahead to
the proximity of death.

Simple

Roses are red.

Violets are blue.

You are sexy.

And who needs a rhyme when you look

this drop-dead gorgeous.

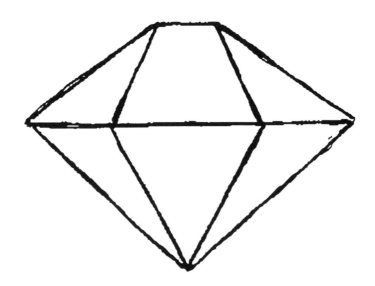

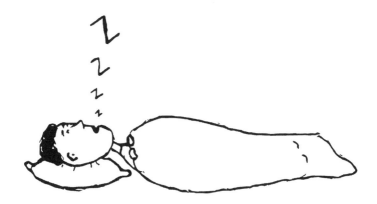

Lazy

Yes, I have gumption. Yes, I can fully function.
Yes, I am competent. Yes, I have accomplishments.
It's just that, mmm, y'know, I'm really into
being lazy right now.

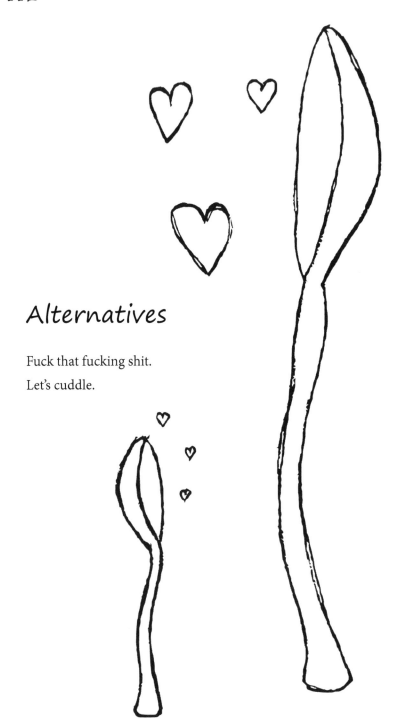

Alternatives

Fuck that fucking shit.

Let's cuddle.

Insomnia

Chatty, scratchy paws and bratty, catty calls
deafen – speak always when inappropriate.
Domestic animals, I haven't yet met them all,
but mine deter my rest, desperate for a pet.

Masculinity

Masculinity is a farce. A ridiculous scam.

Dudes can most definitely cry.

Sad movies tug at my heart, and my meticulous dam
can't keep the tears from my eyes.

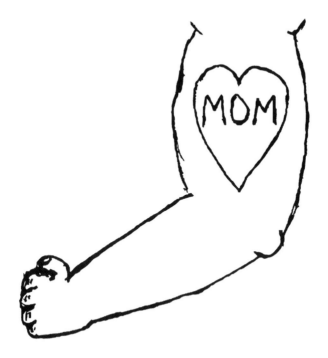

Viewer Discretion

She calls me on the phone for a ride. She has no means.
I take her back to her place. She gets down on both knees.
I need to see that body of hers. I get her out of those jeans.
We move it to the bed. I got her yelling out yes please.

Subjective

A middle finger is the most honest thing out there.
Don't trust a peace sign. They are far from rare.
You don't see the second finger much, but when you do,
you know wholeheartedly what it means: F to the U.
Peace signs, though, they never truly mean peace.
They're an overused and flashy and fake centerpiece.
They're backhanded and incredibly subjective.
Put down that first finger and show what you really
want projected.

Carefree

Seriously, don't take life too seriously.

Ha ha ha ha.

Go on and live it fearlessly.

Fa la la la.

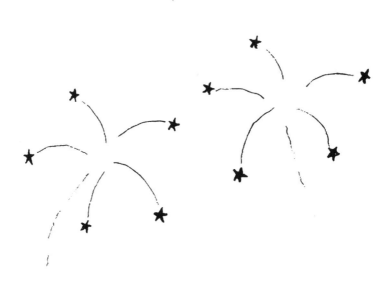

Don't Wanna Know

I don't like thinking about my parents having sex.

Make way, I need to throw up!

It's a little unsettling, if little meant profoundly.

But I do know when they had sex.

It's a matter of subtracting nine months.

September birth means January fuck.

Here comes the liquid vomit!

I was probably conceived on New Year's Eve.

I'm dry-heaving at this point!

Let's raise a glass of champagne to 19-fucking-97.

Inspiration

I crave the idea of inspiring others.
It's what I'd do if I could do anything at all.
I want to show people their capabilities,
whether those are large or small.

Food

I would love a fresh thot pocket
sided with some crispy tater thots.
I would also enjoy a juicy thot dog
dipped in creamy chicken thot pie.
Freudian slips, huh.
Seems like I have something on the brain.

Childhood

My grandpa once told me about his difficult childhood.
I couldn't fathom life in his little neighborhood.
Walking to school through weather cold and warm.
Dropping out to labor on his family's farm.
He regrets having left his education unfinished.
The light of his dreams still flickers,
but it's drastically diminished.
Yet kids today drop out because things are too challenging.
They don't work for their dreams. It's incredibly maddening.

But they don't really know what challenging is.
Around an age like mine, my grandpa went to war.
He struggled to cope with the immediate future in store.
His thoughts centered on home and nothing more.

How could I ever survive in such a daunting position?
I couldn't, because possessing that strength
must require a certain predisposition.
These people come into the world ready to survive,
shooting for the moon and stars until they arrive.
They will never quit no matter the cost.

Pair of Pears

Is this a euphemism for my nutsack?

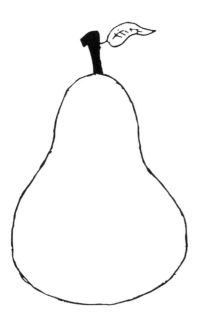

Famous

Do whatever is necessary to be famous.
You've always wanted this, so don't blame us
for throwing away your name
and setting aside your shame.
You do whatever you have to for fame.

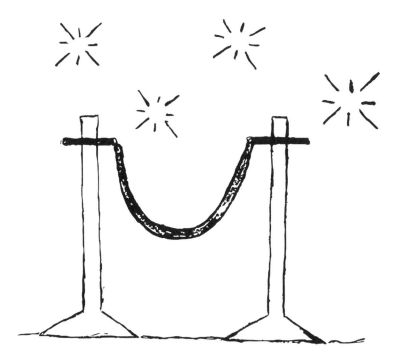

Chest

Bury away your pain and problems and fears.
Bury them in a chest and wrap it in a thick tarp.
Bury that chest deep in the ground and leave it there.
Let it grow thick with dirt like some time capsule.
Never open that Pandora's box of issues.

Finals (Before)

Cram hard for those finals.
Cram hard.
Learn all that stuff you didn't know before
or knew and threw away once you no longer needed it.
Pencil in those tiny, hand-cramping bubbles.

Finals (After)

Congratulations! You've survived!
Let's do it again in a few months.
No showering for a week.
Brushing your teeth like twice.
Sleeping a sum of seven hours over those days.
Crying into your pillow daily.
Yes. Paradise.

Trust

I liked you and loved you,
but I won't try to trust you.
You lost that a long time ago
when you first told me to go.
I don't let my emotions show.
You're not worth my time anymore.

Panera Trip

Panera is literally heaven on Earth.
There is no exaggeration in that statement.
I get a chicken noodle bread bowl
because, fuck, it gives me a mouth orgasm.
Desperate for the fluffy taste of carbs,
I treat myself to a side of bread.
The cashier had the audacity to laugh at me.
Like, the fuck, *Terry?*
This is Panera Bread, is it not?
Even if I wanted a bread bowl of bread with
a side of bread topped with bread-based bread,
you'd better give all that to me without a smirk.
Okay, *Terry?*

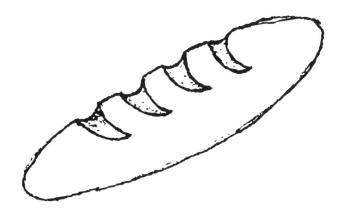

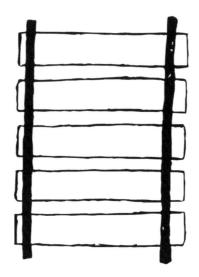

Trains

Trains are the shiiiiiiiit!
Like those mofos blow smoke
and ride the rails like a hobo,
but with a purpose and on an
agreed-upon schedule.

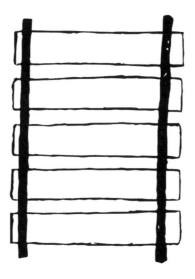

Hair

Having tangles in hair is an infuriating thing.
The pain of pulling and tugging at those knots.
Multiply that pain by ten when those hairs
belong to your ass crack and you have to extract
clumpy balls of toilet paper and shit.

Geriatrics

I love watching Jerry's tricks.
Jerry is a hairy geriatric.
He does some geriatric shit,
showing his flexibility with geriatric splits.
And, believe me, he takes mighty, geriatric shits,
leaving them for others like a merry, sadist prick.
Jerry can suck a...well, just think.

Runaway

Never threaten to run away.

Your parents will wait for you to stand by your word,

even if you have a duffel bag packed and everything.

Maybe they don't care if you leave.

Maybe they know you're just desperate for attention.

Nostalgia

I didn't use to swear...

...so much.

My Way

It's hard to write like old poets did, so I won't try.
I don't seduce with my words like Shakespeare
nor do I beat with your heart like Milton
nor do I take uncharted steps like Frost.
I write like myself, and we'll see where that gets me.

Funny

I'm not funny.
Please don't call me that.
I occasionally make jokes,
but, really, I'm just blowing smoke
to hide the fact that I'm not happy.
Please don't call me happy.

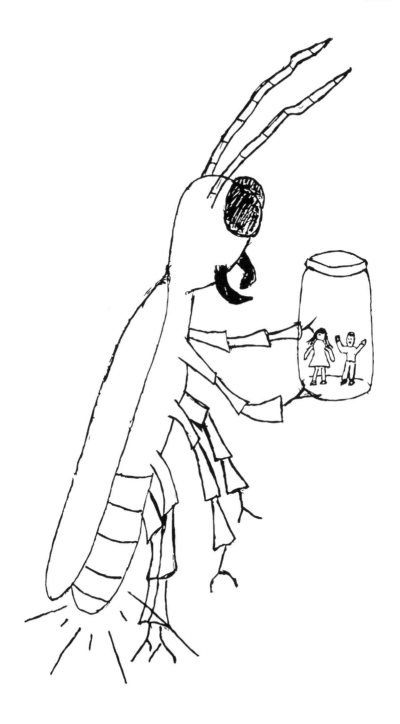

Forgotten

Simpler rhymes and simpler times.
Tiny words and spiny verbs
forgotten on those tilted curbs,
exchanged for something more
dignified and expressive.
Not so vulgar and suggestive.

Window

Stare out the window and see the world unfold.
Look at buildings spilling and city streets filling
with all the people milling about.
They carry wonders and secrets untold.

There is much to see beyond this thin pane of glass.
Flocks of birds flying and bushy trees dyeing
and everything complying to nature's way.
All these things will eventually come to pass.

This three by six quadrant of wondrous delight
allows a perfect view of things also askew
under the sun's light and sky's soft blue.
That's why it looks much better at night.

English

I don't get English.
I speak and read and write it,
but I literally can't comprehend half the shit in it.
French is the language of love.
German is the language of anger.
Spanish is the language of...something. I'll look into it.

Those languages I don't know, but I somehow understand
the language of incomprehensible, idiomatic expressions;
silly grammatical rules; and odd figurative language –
at least enough to write semi-decent poems.
So, I must ask you,
why the hell would anyone want to learn English?

Euphemism

Lay her across the table gently.

Spread her apart slowly and carefully.

Layer over every inch of her tanned body

until you make her whole again.

Squeeze and caress her suppleness.

Salivate at the thought of tasting her edges.

Tickle her overflowing creases with your finger.

What a delicious peanut butter and jelly sandwich.

Party Time

Hours one through four are titillating and tantalizing.
Your lucid eyes and mind are blurry and thick with booze.
Writhing bodies of girls grind against you
as you suppress the urge of ecstasy in your pants –
a sensual feeling of freedom and presence in this
moment of awesomeness, with stomachs coated warm
and inhibitions running rampant in the nude.

Hours five through eight are treacherous and destructive
and vile as you meet poor liquor again.
This time, it's coagulated in a liquidy bile.
Throats become raw with a painful, acidic burn,
crutched by your excessive intake.
You reminisce of unappreciated times of sobriety yet feel
pressured with the haunting words of *Rally, Rally, Rally...*

God

I like to think that there's a God – that all of this didn't just happen by accident. There's so many intricate and fascinating and undiscovered parts of us people and this world that it seems far too good to be true that an unquantifiable number of atoms just happened to smash together in the right way. Even more, it makes the shitty parts of life a little less shitty knowing there's a purpose to them.

Mind Reader

I want to read minds to know what people think of me.
Then, maybe, I could finally fix myself.

Sex

Sex is far from just physical.
If you want that, then fuck. Fuck hard.
Sex is more than your two bodies pressed
against each other in frictional heat.
It's a mental and emotional and spiritual
fulfillment feeling a person in and out.
It's for the mind and the heart and the soul.

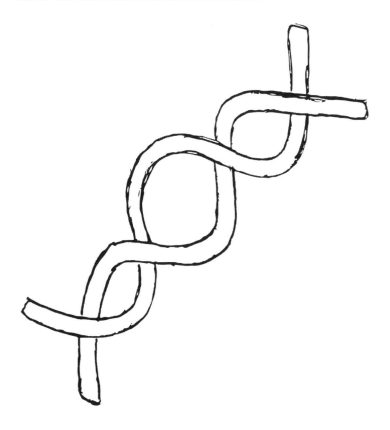

Youth

I don't often connect with kids my age.
"The youth," I say, as I feel a clear divide between us.
They say college holds the best years of your life.
They said that about high school, too.
I didn't feel that then, and I don't feel it now.

I don't have many friends. Not nearly as many as others.
They party while I study.
They talk and laugh while
I sit quietly in the corner of the room, listening.
They make up a social circle while I make up a social dot,
if even that.

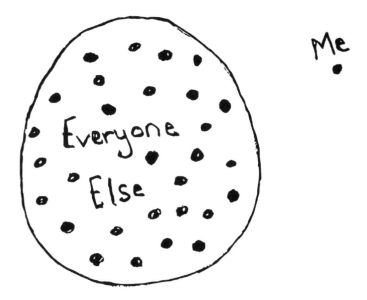

Dessert

Stretch my legs open wide
and lick my booty hole like
a dog lapping up water.

Nature

Those curves are like rounded mountains
that I want to climb night and day.
I'm desperate for your nature's fruit.
It tastes sweet and salty under the rain.
We're tangled together like vines
wrapped around trees.

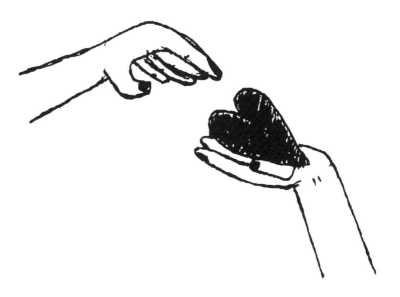

Please You

I am amicable and malleable.
I will bend over for you and
send over more to you.
I aim to please you
and, please you, I do.

Goodbye

I love rewatching series finales of TV shows
just to get a waterfall of tears on
because goodbyes are the hardest.

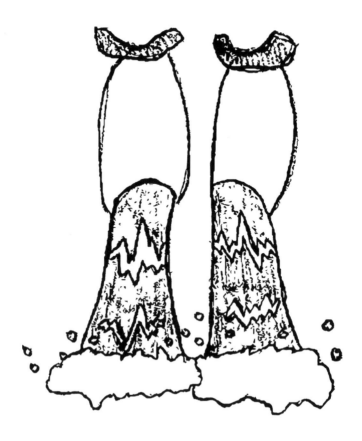

Thing

I make good points about things,
like remember that time that I
suggested that thing and we did it
and we had so much fun? See?

Polished

I've seen a turd polished before,
so don't lie when you say you can't be better.

Candlestick

I am a candlestick.
You burn me slowly and deliberately
like a twisted arsonist,
watching me pool around your feet
and resolidify but now as a deformed
mess of wax of what I used to be.

Heights

Heights don't really scare me.
At least, they shouldn't from an evolutionary standpoint.
Somehow, though, I am afraid from a mental perspective.
Looking over an edge – even standing atop a ladder –
sends a wave of nausea and vertigo through my bones.
I think it's from something unrelated to the height factor.

Falling would be exhilarating for the seconds it lasted.
I'm sure I'd even love it,
if it weren't for the finite abruptness of hitting the ground
and what happens when body meets pavement.
The immediacy of death.
That frightens me and,
more so, the uncertainty of what comes after.

Write

Write because you want to,
not because you have to.
There's beauty and magic in it then.

Addicted

Give me some of it. Gimme gimme.
Just one more hit and then I'll quit.
I promise.
I need that nicotine. That adrenaline rush.
That calming buzz. That blissful hush.

I need it because the world seems so bleak
and painful and pointless when you're away.
Without you, I'm so weak.
Wifi, come back to stay.

Geraldine

Geraldine is mean
and, quite frankly, obscene.
Wherever she goes, she makes a scene,
adding fuel to fires like kerosene.
No wonder she has no friends.
Skanky, cranky 'ol Geraldine.

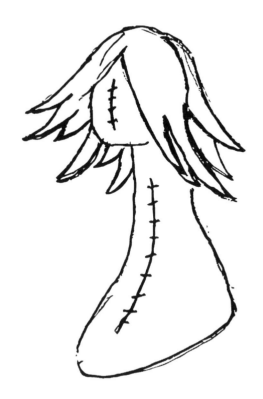

Painting

I stare awestruck at her delicate features
like I would a painting.
Neurons jump like frenzied grasshoppers
as my mind examines each intricate detail.
The artist is not present to describe His work.
I doubt I could handle His explanation anyway.

I am left making my own interpretations –
theories that cannot fully encapsulate the wonder of
this masterpiece.
I know it's beautiful. No one needs to tell me that.
Blessed with eyes, I can see it.
Blessed with touch, I can feel it.
Blessed with a heart, I can love it.

The harder I look and the more I seek clarity –
for the complete picture – the more I distort it.
Reluctantly, I lengthen the distance between us.
The masterpiece shrinks in my field of vision
and, with it, comes seemingly less detail.

Human instinct has taught me to press for
answers – to uncover and understand.

Yet this masterpiece has taught me otherwise.
I want to know all about it up close, but
the simplistic nature of looking from afar and
admiring without truly knowing all the answers
that lie inside make it even more beautiful.
This masterpiece of His, I love it.

Sewer

Under the asphalted ground exists a cesspool town.
A damp and wonderful place of goop and poop
where you can dance around.

Clinging to you are mixtures of excrement galore,
carried and crashing against this putrid shore.
Play and splash away your joyful, poop-filled day.
And, if you like it, come back tomorrow for more.

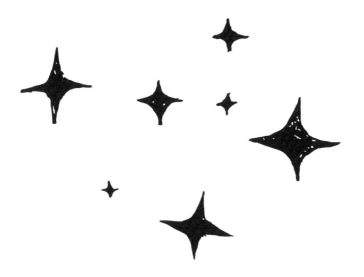

Dreams

Dreams are stupid ideas we
make up with our mind.
Grow up and realize you need to
leave those childish things behind.

They won't take you anywhere,
these imagined scenarios of yours.
Get a job, punch your timecard,
be an adult, and leave at four.

Parenting

I'm desperately afraid of fatherhood.
I'm afraid of having that responsibility.
In no way am I saying I don't want to be a dad.
I do. Absolutely, I do.
Mentoring my son. Protecting my daughter.
I want to, but what if I suck so bad at it?
I don't want to suck.
I can't afford to fail at that.

That's not something I worry about with my wife, though.
No, I don't have one yet, but I know who she is –
who she will be.
I know she'll be amazing.
If that's all I know in life, I know it for sure.
I'll observe her and help her and
learn from her ways.
I hope to come even the slightest
bit close to her perfection.

Make Me

Juniper leaves
and comfy sleeves
make me feel happy.

Romantic love
and cuddles and hugs
make me feel sappy.

Stomach sickness
and condescending prickness
make me feel crappy.

The pitter-patter of rain
and books by Mark Twain
make me feel nappy.

Perfectly sculpted bums
and hand-sized bosoms
make me feel fappy.

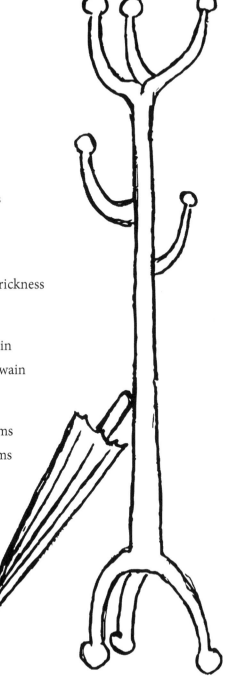

Rejection

I've never felt the feeling of being dumped before.
To be fair, the girls I've seriously dated total four.
But now that I'm with the right person,
I don't worry about this happening anymore.

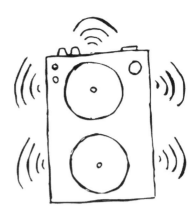

Vibe

That beat bumps and your feet stomp
to that bass drum and those guitar strums.
Feel young and look dumb,
plumb drunk on some plum rum.
Loosen up some and have some fun.
Bum it and come from home.
Don't be glum. Get numb from my plug
for buds and thrum along with the buzzing hum.

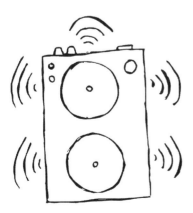

Bathroom

There were three empty urinals
in the boy's bathroom.
Marcus took the middle one and
made everyone else feel uncomfortable.

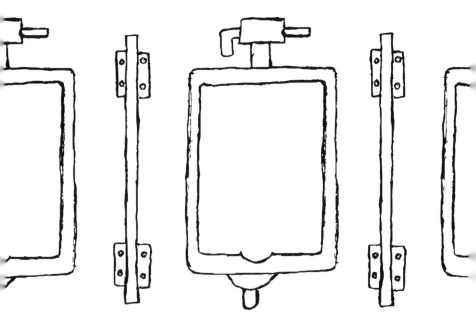

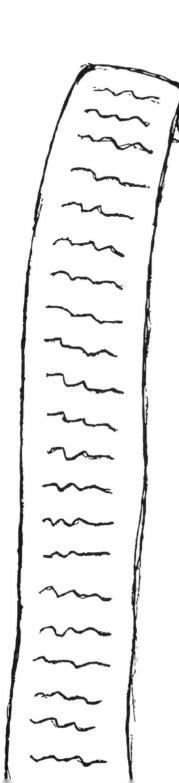

Rules

Suit up.
Strip down.
Muscle up.
Slim down.
Liquor up.
Get down.
The collage
of rules for college,
guys and girls,
respectively.

Silence

Silence will always be your friend.

It will always be there for you.

At times, it's socially aware when you're in a conversation.

It waits patiently in the corner, in silence.

Other times, it's intrusive and overpowers

your ears with a high-pitched whining,

demanding your attention.

Silence is a little fickle,

but it'll be the only thing to enter the void with you.

Stop Talking

My one friend suggested sticking his dick in a blender.
Another wanted someone to snort cocaine off his dick.
I'm stuck wondering how I ended up with friends
focused on doing unheard of things to their genitals.

Attire

If I'm dressed up, don't trust I'm having a good day.

If I'm dressed down, don't trust I'm having a mood day.

Don't assume anything from my clothes.

If you want to know, just ask me how it goes.

Sleep, Darling

Close your eyes and sleep, my darling.

Tomorrow will bring you better things.

Your pain from today has been felt.

Your weeps have been heard.

Your tears have dried.

Hush, darling.

Rest your head and heart and tongue.

Go to sleep, and, when you wake,

you'll see what I mean.

Hey, Siri

I snake between the crowd of zombified people,
spying their absent expressions and glassy looks.
But, mostly, it's napes of necks and tops of heads
with the occasional bald spot and tightly knit man-bun.
Eyes peer down, certainly not boring holes into the ground.
What enjoyment would erroneous cracks in cement bring?

Right arms (left, for the weirdos) are crooked,
angled inward toward their sternums.
It seems like a painful and awkward position.
What they hold lacks any physical weight,
but, in capability and compatibility, it's immense.
It fits us perfectly.

From above, we must look like determined ants,
marching in blissful and simplistic synchronicity.
Or, maybe, more like those little, home-cleaning robots –
bumping, stopping, recalculating, and constantly moving.
We rarely slow as we progress toward our destinations.

I feel strange with my erect posture and directional stare.
I assimilate, tilting my head down at forty-five degrees.
The luminescent blue reflects brightly against my eyes.
Scrolling. Tapping. Pretending I'm doing something.

...

...

Ouch!
Hey, Siri, why didn't you warn me about the tree?
Stop.
Recalculate.
Keep going.

Sneezes

Whenever it does that light drizzle spritz crap outside,
it feels like I'm being hit by persistent sneeze spit.

Listen

Would you even listen if I didn't swear so much?

If I didn't care so much?

Or wear so much fancy crap?

It's all about perception,

and you are my reception.

You see me as important.

A view I see as distorted.

Elevator

There is a special place in Hell for elevator chumps.
People who ride it to the second floor.
People who press all the buttons.
People who squeak out a fart and
let it choke us in this metal box.
People who talk when we all know
awkward silence is the unspoken rule.
Just go! Get out of this elevator
before I send you to Hell myself.

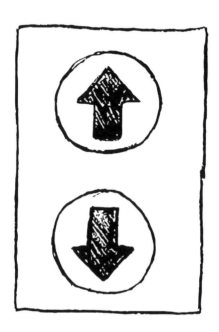

Float

Bobbing in the sea of
possibilities like a stagnant buoy,
you feel more like an iceberg.
90% of your body is submerged,
and the remaining 10% is exposed and
left fighting to breathe strained breaths.

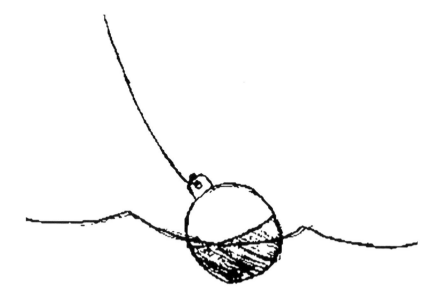

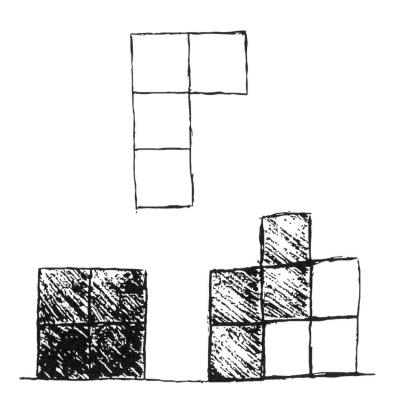

Autocorrect

Autocorrect can really duck you over.

God ducking dammit!

I'm done with this shot!

Blobs

Let's all be blobs.
I'd be a plush, putty-material, blue blob
because blue is my favorite color.
A faceless, nameless, limbless blob
not worried about his body.
I'd simply blob around with my other blob friends.
A world of blobs with nothing to do
but bask in the glory of our blobbiness.

Decipher

Can you write me an algorithm to understand people?
I'll buy it from you because
my brain isn't doing a good enough job
figuring them out itself.

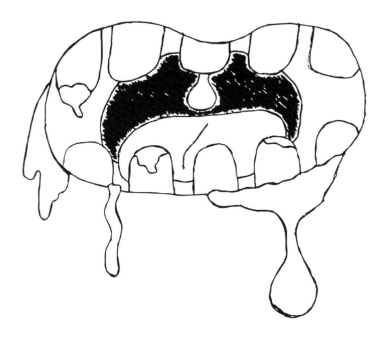

White Condiments

White condiments (and dressings) are disgusting,
at least in how they look. I've never eaten them.
Mayo, ranch, and tartar sauce all make me want to vomit.
I was scarred by an image during second-grade lunch,
watching a plump, young fella stuff his face with salad,
it drenched in ranch that covered his thick lips.
It never leaves my mind.

Mural

A mural of poop is a mural nonetheless,
but, instead of elegance, it elicits a dreadful mess.
Every day the artist would carefully grease
the wall with another layer of stinky feces.

Your putrid artwork demands a bath in Purell.
Drew, I explicitly asked you to make a beautiful mural.
Like one with paint or glass, not something so earthy.
Not something from the horse stables at the local derby.

No, you can't finish your highly irregular masterpiece.
Now I understand what you meant by eccentric artist.
You've ruined our school lobby by staining our entry wall.
Leave this school and return to your day-job at the mall.

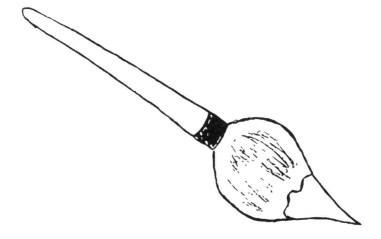

Drive

Driving into the sunset is such an odd phrase.
You'll never physically reach that point.
Try to and you'll just keep rounding
the Earth's vast circumference.
Like us all, you're stuck here forever
in this vacuum world.

Cereal

A bowl of cereal can be a bowl of ethereal,
if you have the right mind to choose the right kind.
Those colorful Frooty Loops –
just like a colder, crunchier, and fruitier soup.
Bouncing around the bowl like bumper car things.
They're pinging; delectable; and tasty, little rings.
Swish around the speckled milk with your spoon.
But eat quick because its eclectic taste is gone by noon.

Or you could be lame and eat some other cereal,
enjoying processed flakes or crisps of cardboard material.
A rainbow of flavor, with each loop there is a surprise.
Nothing else will make your morning self feel alive.
Oh, look, you went and ate the whole box gone.
The near future better come with cereal that respawns.

Staring

The act of staring takes a lot of concentration
and commitment.
Stare until the world turns purple and then to
shades of black and gray.
Stare until your eyes get tired and your eyelids
become restless and desperate for closure.
Stare until a thick film of dust coats your eyes
because your eyelashes haven't flicked shut for hours.
Stare until color and the objects you observe no
longer have meaning.
Stare until your other senses have shut down
because you're focusing all your attention on sight.
Stare at that thing, unless that thing is a person
and you're a serial killer scoping out your next victim.

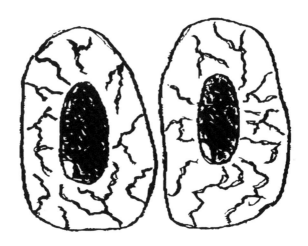

Symbol

I do not represent a symbol of any kind.

Don't idolize me, if you do.

I don't promote anything,

and I will never tell you what to do.

I'm a simple human being like everyone else.

I have my opinions, but I keep them to myself.

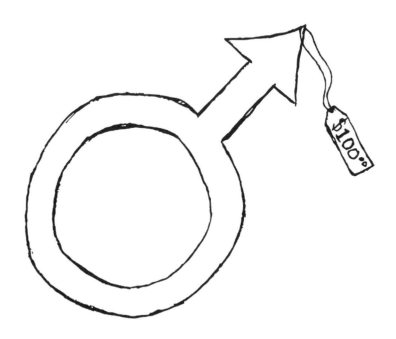

Sin

Sin. Sin. Sinning is fun.
Grin. Grin. Grinning at the nun.

An alcohol slip-n-slide
and water guns of cyanide
are my only kryptonite.

Get nude in a pool of jell-o
or fluffy, puffy marshmallow
while snorting some Mello Yello.

Be a toilet arsonist
and then fart and kiss
in a bowl of star citrus.

Spit in that kid's trumpet.
Lick all the crumpets.
Punch that guy's puppet.

Sin. Sin. Sinning is fun.
Grin. Grin...
...uh, the nun downed some liquor
and popped some meds
to forget all the things that were just said.

Time Travel

Ask me if I want to see the past or future
and you'll receive a resounding vote for the past.
My future will come soon enough, so there's
no need to see it before it arrives.
No, I wouldn't make the slightest of
changes to my past.
Conditional on whether I'd rip apart
the space-time continuum, I'd meet
myself and shake his hand –
his left because I know where the
right has been –
just to tell him to keep doing what he's doing
because he ends up landing a babe.

Alone

The cobwebbed corner shields me with plaster walls.
This sanctified place from when I was younger
has gotten very little use in the past few years as
I steeled myself to the world.
But She sees me again and will on a regular basis.
Daily meet-and-greets as I'm coddled gently.
Inevitable that Death play tag with Life, but, sadly,
He tagged someone I loved.

I talk to Her and ask Her for answers.
Do I expect anything besides beige silence?
Coldness has mixed with my blood, giving way to
a shriveled and frostbitten heart surrounded
by an encasement of icy tears.
Fuck you, Death. Fuck you with a vengeance
and destruction that only you could dole out.
Take someone else – absolutely anyone else.
I mean that with no sincerity or seriousness.
Don't take anyone else. Leave us all alone.

Devoid of feeling I am.
No past thoughts can bring happiness.
No painful thoughts can bring more pain.
No sad thoughts can drain anything more from me.

She takes my nails with no complaint,
letting me express myself as necessary.
My parents worry as I've not eaten in days
and move very little and murmur responses.

I just want this corner.
That is the only solace that helps right now.
She'll see me through my recovery
and bring me back to where I need to be.

Goodbye, you bearer of my heart.

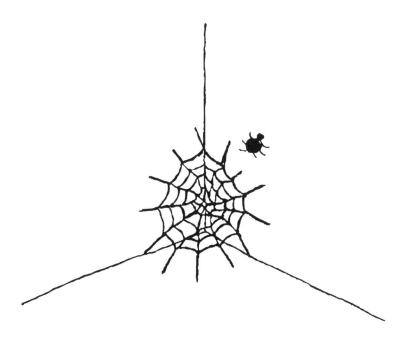

Smile

Apple peels and tender strips of beef
pocket themselves in between your teeth.
Feel around in there with a toothpick.
Dig 'em out, get 'em out, and give 'em a good flick
right in the face of that flighty tooth fairy thief.

Impossible

I bestow upon you an impossible task.
Paraphrase your life for me.
Summarize it in a 100-word abstract.
Capture all your highlights in life.
If you have none, then 100 words
shouldn't be as challenging to meet.
And if you have many,
give me the bare essentials
so I can have a quick rundown of you.
Avoid that extraneous crap
because I know you barely care about it,
so I definitely won't care about it either.

Words

Words began as meaningless, guttural sounds,
until, one day, some overachiever found
a way to mash them together to make coherent chunks
so that those throaty grunts and chicken clucks
started flowing like peppy, cheerleader spunk.

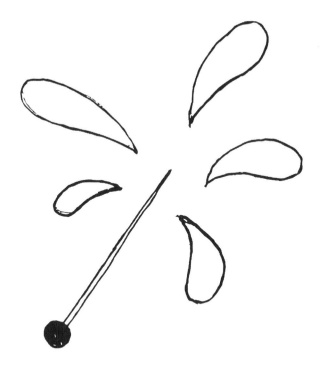

Loss of Innocence

I grew up way too fast.
I was secluded all my life –
lived in the same place –
knew the same people –
had the same experiences.
All too quickly, I was thrust into everything.
And, honestly, the world outside
my bubble sucks.

Barista by Day, Bartender by Night

You are like a superhero,
breathing life into one personality and identity
during the day and another at night.
You are also unlike a superhero
as you lack the certain conviction
and passion for crime-fighting and overall ability
that those spandexed crusaders have.
You do have the mask,
though, for your bar's theme:
Anonymous Encounters.

Your morning life is that of barista
at your own coffee shop.
You slide saucers of steaming liquid coffee grounds
and misspell customers' names on to-go cups.
As the sun sets on another benign day, your
counter of mountained pastries and bean-juice drinks
are replaced by a sea of bottles with waves
of brown or clear liquid.
You become bartender, cracking jokes and
toweling off the same glass cup in front of your patrons.

A one-stop shop of caffeine injection
for a productive, energized day
and alcohol depressant for a productive night's rest.
Repeat the cycle every 24 hours.
Your money matters to us.

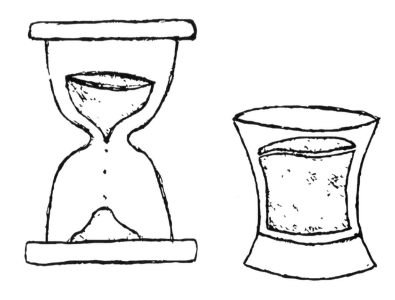

Time

What's more callous than Time?
He'll let good days pass like seconds
but force painful minutes to feel like hours
or, worse, years.
He's got a deal with Death,
exchanging you for the amount on
your price tag.
He's stingy with doling more time out,
only giving you some when he chooses.
All the while, he passes his own time
by spinning his giant hourglass.

Topics of Conversation

I can't talk to people.
I really suck at it.
My brain unplugs itself from my tongue,
bids me farewell with a few parting words,
and hibernates till we're alone again.
Like a crappy football player,
I fumble –
fumble for topics of conversation.

This weather we're having, huh...
...it's something else, isn't it?
Y'know, clouds and wind and sun.
Nature is really crushing it.

Indifference

I feel so indifferent about a lot of things.
What if I don't finish this poem?
Eh, don't care.

Love

How do you tell someone you love them?
Mushy feelings, bleh.

Holidays

The holiday season is the best time of the year.
There is no better feeling than when it draws near.
Holidays put me in a holi-daze –
something that never fails to amaze me.

Good food and happy moods pair nicely
with folly jolly and lots of holly and peppermint tea.
Mistletoe and Christmas snow and ho ho ho
give a magical quality.

And when it's up and gone away,
I'm left waiting 364 more days
for old, fat Santy Clause
and his packed, red sleigh.

Your Period

Your period belongs to you.
It's personal to you
because it comes from you
and is just as old as you.
Red mud as red as blood because it is blood sludge.
Your period is not something new.

My period is not unique,
and it's not a commencement.
A minuscule, black dot that I sneak
in at the end of this sentence.

Conscience

I wish I had a less conscientious conscience.
It's stopping me from doing all this cool stuff.
I can't think of an example right now,
but you know what I mean.

Crisis

I have a different crisis on a daily basis.
Some are small and some are tall
(for rhyming purposes).
Today, it was sticky, as I accidentally
shampooed with syrup. Icky.

Friends

You think your friends define you,

but they'll sometimes undermine you.

You want status and popularity

and high school and college prosperity.

Just know, you don't need them in your life.

Be happy with your family, husband, or wife.

Or even on your own

because, before we know people,

we all start out alone.

Observe

I observe the world,
preferring that to engaging in it.
I notice your awkward interactions with friends,
your feelings of inadequacy
that you hide with self-deprecating jokes.
I see the mustard stain under your *ear*, for some reason;
the crust in the corner of your eye;
your nervous lip twitch.
I detect all these physical things and
somewhat emotional things in others,
but I fail to recognize them in myself.

Outfit

A patterned vibe from a tattered hide.
Thicker knickers and stockings and smockings.
Flared jeans and outfits like Queen.
This was the fashion of the past.

A tight sweater vest with a soft leather crest.
Elbow pads of tweed emblazoned with a creed.
Long shirts and short skirts,
with skinny jeans and everything in between.
This is the fashion of the present.

Silky, metal mesh infused with our human flesh.
Brass helmet mullets made from casings of bullets.
Frozen, molasses glasses and gel made from krill.
This will be the fashion of the future.

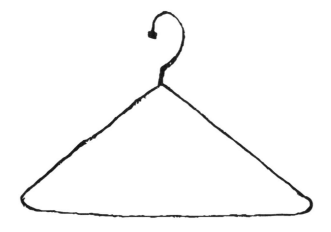

Sleep Walking

Chow down on dog food. Crab walk in the nude.
Climb up the door. Pee on the floor.
On the couch, do a handstand.
Don't you slouch – mimic a nightstand.
Compose a song and sing along.
Even look in the mirror and talk.
Wonderfully weird things happen
when you go on a sleep walk.

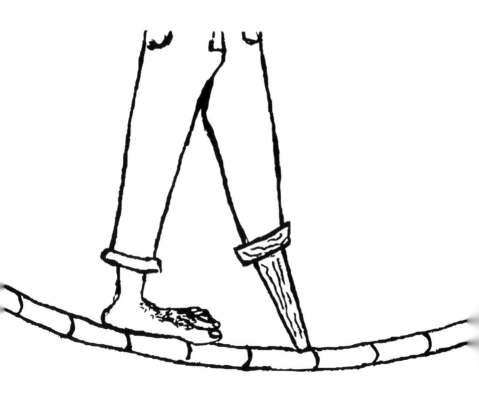

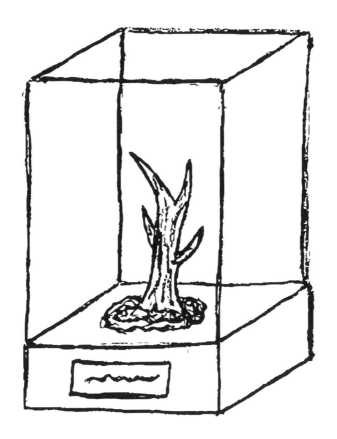

First Crush

She moved away, and it's something that I never got over.
I locked away that part of me in an internal, glass enclosure.

'Rents Confer

Huddled behind the oak door of the classroom
are the teacher and parent(s) of the student.
Things are said. Not really sure what.
No kid has ever been invited.
Secrets to share.
Guess they'll find out when they become
parents themselves.

Speech

Coax and prod and squeeze and push.

Make me face toward the crowd of hush.

A podium for me to stoop.

An Imodium to block my poop.

Weighted eyes and straightened ties

judge in quiet.

I'd rather not speak publicly.

Can I see all of you in private?

Puberty Was Not My Friend

A reflective, metal grip on my catawampus whites.
Red bumps of acne sprouting as clear as daylight.
Earthquake cracks in my confused voice box –
some like light pebbles and others like big rocks.
Wear my boot-cut jeans and tan cargo shorts.
Put on a cringy smile and laugh with a snort.
Spectacles so thick, like heavy window panes.
It was not by choice that from sex I did abstain.

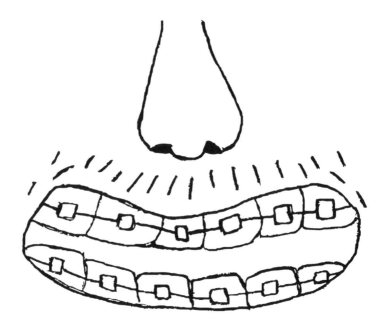

Suit

Eating anywhere accompanies a potential risk.
You could be fine or have pants filled with poop bisque.
Unfortunately, I was not beyond the reach of said sitch –
lovely, lovely food poisoning from a simple sandwich.

On my own in D.C. and without a toilet in reach,
I sprinted for a building, squeezing tight my rear cheeks.
Things spiraled downward.
My stomach pushed further against my butt.
Shit literally happened...in my expensive suit...
fuuuuuuuuuuuuuuck...

I washed my pants in a bathroom sink
and stashed them in a sealed bag.
A week later, when I returned home,
I unzipped it and held back a gag.
It (obviously) smelled like week-old shit.
I thanked my suit for its service and burned it in my fire pit.

Money

Money is not something that you should let
control you or your life.
Really, money is just crinkled, green,
feces-and-cocaine-covered paper.
If we all one day chose to denounce
money, it would be as worthless
as the paper it's printed on.
Make money to live.
Don't live to make money.

Normal

You shouldn't have to be a celebrity to be loved.
I'll cherish and adore you enough
to make it feel like you have millions of fans.
Your normality is what I love the most.

End

It's a well-established fact that nothing lasts forever.
Everything eventually ends – good or bad –
and crumbles to clumps of particulate dust
taken away by circulating winds.

Those good and pure and wonderful things are
a rare beauty to this world, so we claw at them to
come back as they float away through our fingers.

The voids in our brain and heart are poorly refilled with
an agonizing emotion called longing.
Fickle in its definition. Sometimes it lets us reflect
fondly on the time before happiness, that lovely gal, left.
Other times, it forces us back to the same conclusion
that we are not the same without her.

Funny enough, even those bad, ugly, and tragic things
possess a nostalgic property – weird as it may be.
Amidst all that frustration or pain or whatever,
we wish nothing more than its absence.
But when it's left us, nostalgia rears his wistful head again.

The last page, maybe.

Final Thoughts (not a poem)

Thank you, reader whose name I do not know. Thank you for making it this far, or for skipping all or some of the poems and checking out this part of the book, or for choosing to read this current sentence at all. You're the reason I do this. Actually, that's a lie. I do it to make myself laugh, and this book just happened to be a product of that narcissistic, self-indulging tendency. Hopefully you found a reason to laugh, smile, smirk, or breathe slightly out of your nose. I hope you also learned something. That something being, "Wow, this guy is weird, but I would definitely read another book of his poems or anything else he writes." Awww, thank you so much for saying that. Your words mean the world to me. Well, not really. Again, I don't know who you are, and your thoughts are stuck inside your head, and saying these things to these pages won't magically get them to me. Send me a letter at [address omitted] or don't. Now, I leave you with one last thing to consider. As they say in…well, everywhere…what the fuck are you looking at?

But, sincerely, thank you.

Goodbye.

Acknowledgements

1. My thanks and appreciation to my high school English teacher, Mr. Ward, for teaching me what poetry can be and do.

2. More thanks to him for understanding that, instead of writing poetry as he showed me, I decided to write stuff like this. Sorry.

3. My gratitude to the one I dedicated this book to for always encouraging me, reading my poems, and being a constant source of inspiration.

4. My thanks to my parents for tolerating my need to do this whole writing thing despite, I'm sure, thinking, "Please let this foolishness stop." You keep me grounded. My love to you both.

5. My thanks to the people who read my early drafts and laughed along with me and maybe even thought I had something loose in my head. I promise I don't.

6. Et cetera thanks to et cetera people.

The actual last page.

Until next time.

Me

Corey Caskey is tall like a basketball player. He is bespectacled like Benjamin Franklin and a majority of the population. He is a man with proportional feet and has a knack for scribbling words with his left hand. He is a budding writer working to turn his passion and eccentric thoughts into an adequately sized book (this one)! Self-published, Corey is looking to politely push, nod, and smile his way into the world of authorship. With his accurate, insightful, hilarious, and humble introspections, he feels personally connected to these poems that are full of language only a distant mother could love, and he knows you'll feel connected to them, too.

Made in the USA
Columbia, SC
02 June 2019